Geography of Loss

8/6/21

Gerda,
May your path be
abundant with light,
love + laughter...

Judith Prest

poems by

Judith Prest

Finishing Line Press
Georgetown, Kentucky

Geography of Loss

ACKNOWLEDGMENTS

Gratitude to the following anthologies and journals for publication of these poems.

Allowing Grace appeared in *Beloved on the Earth, Layers of Possibility*, and *Peer Glass*
Wardrobe Alchemy   appeared in *Up the River, and will appear in Quillkeepers Press Parenting Anthology*
Coming to Grips appeared in *Up the River*
Now & Then, **Gates**, and **Steel** appeared in *Fredericksburg Literary & Art Review*
Summer 1966: Vietnam Conflict Escalates appeared in *The Akros Review*
Litany for Survival (Excerpt) appeared in *We'Moon.*
Monumental appeared in Rockvale Review
What I Want appeared online in *Writers Resist* and in *Black Lives Matter: Poems for a New World,* published in the UK.

Deep gratitude to Linda Leedy Schneider, poet, writing teacher and friend, who worked with me to edit my work for this book.

Publisher: Leah Huete de Maines
Editor: Christen Kincaid
Cover Art: Judith Prest
Author Photo: Ashley Holley
Cover Design: Elizabeth Maines McCleavy

Order online: www.finishinglinepress.com
            also available on amazon.com

Author inquiries and mail orders:
Finishing Line Press
P. O. Box 1626
Georgetown, Kentucky 40324
U. S. A.

Table of Contents

This work is in honor of all my lost dear ones, and for everyone who is living through grief, learning to survive. I hope the reader will find truth and comfort in these words

Loss

Suddenly life churns with brown silt
like a river after a storm.
Dark currents cut channels
rip new pathways
obliterate the banks I knew.

Each step now takes me deeper
no maps, no landmarks even
the stars shrouded.
On the river of loss
we can only navigate by faith.

Grief

Tangled sheets,
night sweats.
A dark rider
tramples sleep,
disturbs
my dreams.

The night visitor arrives,
catapults me from sleep.
I wake,
heart clenched,
peer through
slitted lids,
feel the room roll,
walls bend.

The night traveler
takes me aboard.
Mist obscures
starlight,
erases all hope
of navigation.

Only my conviction
keeps me present,
only my faith
that this ride
will end.

Only my belief
    in the limits of darkness,
        the promise of dawn,
            necessity of surrender,
                inevitability of grace
permit this flight.

Sleepwalk

I sleep and my house transforms.
Stairs collapse, rooms shrink,
trees and bushes grow up,
brush against the asbestos siding
and the leaky roof.

Sleep transports me
to my oldest home,
the one I know
by smell and touch
even in the darkest night.

I sleepwalk
out of the blue bedroom,
along oak floored hallway
into the living room,
straight into the easy chair.
Daddy's ghost
moves over to make room.

But I am too restless to sit.
I rise again,
move through the dining room,
through the cracked plaster archway
into the kitchen where grey linoleum,
new again, is slick enough
to slide on in stocking-feet.
I glide across to the stove
and twirl there until
dizzy overtakes me.

Through sleep's filmy curtain,
I step down, into the "outkitchen",
past the washer and dryer, and
the old dead Westinghouse stove
piled with junk.

I open the purple painted screen door,
pause on the concrete porch to sniff the air.
I listen as katydids racket their way
through this night, walk gently
down cement steps, into the grass.

I circle the house three times,
Passing maple, dogwood, white pine.
Thick air and dark surround me
under sleep's moonless sky,

Waves of whippoorwill, tree frog
and leaf rustle roll over me.
I walk the land, absorb its essence
through bare feet,
then wake wordless
to northern sunlight
through a second story window.

Invisible Geography

When I drive on County Road,
memory's landscape lives in me
invisible geography.
I see the giant gum tree that once
graced Maloney's pasture,
blazing red
in a long-gone late October.
Below the train trestle
a wooden bridge carries the dirt road
across Red Lion Creek – not the soul-less
cement culvert under the
asphalt of now.

When I take 71, south of Red Lion,
up the hill, past
the Hoffecker rental house,
the bloated boxes
of high-end tract houses
dissolve into phantom fields.
I see cows amble uphill
toward the David's big red barn,
smell the manure Bill David used to spread
this time of year.

Further up the road, I sense
dim shapes of horses,
mine and Barby's,
meeting at the fence line;
adjoining pastures,
paths worn
through the hedgerow
now gone over entirely
to multiflora rose and honeysuckle.

Beneath the now,
outlines of ghost trees
stand sentinel,
bear witness.

The Places I Knew

The places I knew have changed.
I lived here, played out my
childhood, my wild-girl years
in these woods and fields.

Once I knew every road and tree,
now I stand,
stunned wordless;
the scene a neon theme park
with no name.

I want to rewind
history like a movie,
snap the film
before the scary part,
join the conspiracy
to protect the young.

I discover that
holding memory
in my hands can fill
a room with pain.

This is the moment
when I know
the acid of fear
will eat my world
if I don't face it.

In Hand

I think it was a spatula.
Dark brown, darker
in the grooves of wood grain
deepened by time.

It hung in my mother's
kitchen on a peg board
with other vintage
kitchen implements,
then rested in a crock
beside my stove.

My great grandmother's spatula;
gone missing, was
my kitchen talisman,
kept watch
over my motley crew
of pots and pans,
spoons and spatulas.

I used it to stir chili
and curries, each time
envisioned Sarah Wolfe
rolling in her grave in Rock Glen
as her wooden spatula,
which had only known
flour, sugar, butter,
vinegar and lard, mingled
with cumin and coriander,
turmeric, cayenne.

I'd hold
this holy relic
in my hand,
imagine Sarah's hand,
so often empty,
like her pockets,

stirring raw fried potatoes
in a cast iron pan.

Hungers

My hands are hungry
for the feel of bread dough.
Palms and fingers
crave the yeasty give of kneading.
The dance of hands
waking the yeast,
the scent
waking memory
to visions of other lives,
in vanished kitchens.

I can see my mother
and her mother and her mother,
endlessly mirrored
along time's hallway,
women who stood
in plain kitchens
making magic
with flour, water and yeast
creating something
from nearly nothing.

My hands are hungry
for the feel of bread dough.
My heart is hungry
for connection
with my grandmothers

2171 Oakdale Avenue, Glenside

In broad daylight I
climb familiar steps,
steep, flanked by ivy
step onto the front porch
look into the living room.
Sunlight glints hard off
newly sealed wood
warm colored walls.

Along a side wall, facing the stairs,
sits the ghost of the hard scratchy couch
       where my mother and I sat in July 1957,
       Grandmother across from us in her rocker
as they and I, not yet six,
struggled to absorb the jolt
of Granddaddy dead
just that morning.

Like a thief,
I open the gate
walk the narrow concrete path
along chain link fence
to the back yard,
peer through
my grandmother's
kitchen window.

It smells of dust now,
not bananas
in Grandma's kitchen—the dark
pantry gone—a glass door
opening to the back garden
where Grandaddy
grew his roses.

My Great Aunt Carrie Speaks at Last

for Carrie Mae Arnold, 1878-1955

I was a woman
who was not fit
who did not fit
the world I was born into
I cast off the binding of
conventions that chafed my spirit
choked my voice--
I traveled from closed
hills of coal and clay
to the open banks of a delta
where rich brown water
poured into a blue blue gulf

I followed the call of the water spirit
to the bottom of the continent
the mouth of a great river
to a place of enchantment
glitter and disguise:
sparkling promise bobbed
on the waters;
turned to tinsel
shards of bright celluloid
that cut me
cut me deep

I returned to the hills
the dark green hollows
of my birth, returned to the fold
took up the yoke, allowed my life
to be plowed into neat rows
I choked on the dust
ached for the shine and sway
the sparkling carnival…

I began to dance within my traces

until I kicked them over
when I could dance no more
I let myself
be put away like a broken doll
I allowed them to set me apart
so I would not spill my bright poison
across their well swept kitchen floors

Monumental

for my great aunt, Carrie Mae Arnold, 1878-1955

Aunt Carrie, who died
in the Allentown Asylum,
the one
who left Nowhere, PA
for vaudeville
in New Orleans,
who returned,
married a failed farmer.

Aunt Carrie, the one
dressed in black,
walked country roads
barefoot, weeping.
Aunt Carrie,
who passed the
wildwoman gene
through my mother
down to me.

I have her photograph,
blown up
from a tiny tintype.
She sits
dolled up, smiles wide.
A dapper man
sits next to her,
back in the day
when folks did not smile
at the camera.

I want to see this image
of my Great Aunt Carrie
in all her glory,
looking like a fancy lady.
I want to see

this photo
thirty feet high
on Main Street
in Allentown.

Lost Language

My mother's
full throated laugh,
the pause as she takes a drag
on her cigarette
on the other end of the phone.

My father's voice
tells a story,
he chuckles,
his blue eyes twinkle.
His "Oh, nuts!"
when he can't get
the old Gravely mower going—again.

My grandmother's
gasp of disapproval
when my mother dyes
her sneakers purple.

The scratchy cacophony
of "The Aunties"
floats up through the heat register
from Nana's living room,
where Barby and I listen.
Sophie, Carrie, Jo and Agnes
all talk at once,
voices like rusty hinges,
encoding family history
into our dreams.

Snake Bite Kit

After my father died,
I found a scarlet metal box
nestled in his sock drawer
surrounded by plain white socks.
The box holds gauze,
a razor blade
to cut the X in the skin,
a rubber cup
to suck out the poison.

My father was an Eagle scout,
a gentle man,
who showed me
how to hold a snake.

What I mean by gentle is his voice
when he read me to sleep.
I never heard him raise it in anger
though he did tell me
he had to knock a man down once.
I forget why.

Dad knew this: **be prepared,**
know how to hold a snake
close behind the head,
keep a snake bite kit
in your sock drawer
in case it turns and bites you.

What I mean is
I always felt safe
around my father because
he could hold me, a snake,
whatever life sent him
in his steady hands.

On Becoming A "Grown-up"

for my father

your hands
in the hospital
thin now
but still huge
one holding mine
through those last nights
anchoring your spirit
in the pause before flight

cold stale air,
florescent light
through the relentless hum
of the night hospital
your voice
faintly tracing
the map of your life
one more time

I see myself then: your daughter
a grown woman
not yet a mother
no longer a girl,
walking with you
to the edge
blinded
by tears and fear

my first lessons on
the immortality of love
as you helped me cross
the last boundary
of childhood

Death Watch

hospital nights
the walls breathe
life's machinery
beeps and blinks
even as death waits
in the corner of the room

we watch for that moment
when the spirit will rise
and it will
even as we reach
our living hands
across the abyss
even as we seek to
follow with our hearts

breath has left with spirit
only your form remains
leaving us forever changed
by our journey with you

In Time

At noon I am asleep
in my parents' bed
buried under the weight
of three nights
at the hospital.
The phone wakes me.
My mother
from the hospital,
"Your father says
he's going to die this afternoon."

I rise from the bed,
stumble to the kitchen
search for the Valiant keys,
dropped god-knows-where
this morning when I came in.
Then I recall the ancient
Chevy that starts
with no key. Halfway
down the rutted lane
a tire goes flat.
Panic warps
time and I reverse hard
up the lane, fly into the house,
begin dialing to beg a ride.
A neighbor comes,
but the needle is on empty
we have to stop for gas.

We arrive. I sprint
up the hospital steps
into the lobby,
into the elevator,
down the hall to my father's room
where he has just finished
his final bowl
of chocolate ice cream.

I arrive in time to hear
my mother say
"It all goes by so fast"
in time to hold his hand
in time to see
his blue eyes close,
to sit silent, in the
sacred space
of his breathing
until his chest is still.

Wardrobe Alchemy

for my mother

Her dress is bold: eye-grabbing yellow
on top, dotted with black.
Billowing black skirt swirls
from hips to calf, flows around her
as she steps from the trolley to the street,
into the bank, out to lunch.

Silky folds slither along the sidewalk,
slide through subway turnstiles,
splashes of yellow and black sashay
down Broad Street.

She sheds all traces of joyless
duty, slips right past
her mother's pointed finger,
predictions of ruin and calamity—she
will dance, will smoke, will play cards,
drink beer in speakeasies—temperance,
corsets and constraints be damned.

In her yellow and black dress
she'll stride across borders, over
the edge of her known world,
breaking trail for me.

Cup with Violets

Mother, I am thinking of
the cup with violets-
your gift:
"I want you to think of me
when you use this."
Those words gave me pause.
Were you tempting fate,
or were you at eighty-something
merely considering
your own mortality?

A large mug, well balanced
sprinkled with violets on white,
rich lavender inside,
lavender handle
your trademark color
sits on the mug shelf
over blue tiled counter,
in my chaotic kitchen
that replicates your own.

I remember your words
each time I choose
the cup with violets,
each time I pour in
morning coffee.
Every time
I lift the violet mug,
I sip the inevitability of loss.

Coming to Grips

When I was a young woman,
before my father died, before
I watched my mother become old
I didn't know I'd see her
lose her words one day.

I didn't know that sitting with her
at the end of her life
would remind me of walking
an endless empty beach
at low tide.

Later, I learned that when
dementia cleans house,
underpants turn up in the freezer
cash in the towel closet. But that is
not how it went with my mother.

Instead she just took flight,
eyes suddenly empty as
a vacant house on a prairie.
One day she just stopped making
sense, turned in on herself.

She was mute.
Fully engaged in the work
of dying, left me
to wash her feet,
appointed me as witness.

Allowing Grace

for Grace Arnold Prest 1917-2002

I dance
balanced on the edge
between worlds,
memories telescope
play simultaneously with dreams
and reality
a festival of images.

I accept death
invite it as a beginning.
I am watching my mother's illusions
collapse around her,
pile high in the hospital bed.
fill the space so she barely has room.
I watch her hang on,
hands clawed with arthritis,
frozen on the wheel of her life
grasping, seeking,
resisting.

I sing lullabies in my head.
I float above the room,
out the window,
between bare branches.
follow the river of migrating blackbirds,
rise with the moon
dance with the wind.

Somewhere the child I was
is wailing.
I grieve the loss of mother
accept that for now
I mother her
and myself as well.

I hold her hands,
feel the bones
so near the surface,
sense her spirit not yet unbound,
release my claim on her being.
release with love,
enduring, dreaming,
dancing with spirit.

I imagine heartbeats:
hers fainter,
mine steady
all centered,
aligned with the universe.
I pray for patience,
pray for endurance,
pray for the gift of
allowing grace.

Grace

for Grace Arnold Prest, June 19, 1917 – March 30, 2002

All day today I am inside,
I stay in the warm room.
The oxygen machine, like a little generator,
creates background noise
that I no longer notice.
My dear ones are nearby,
Alan quietly at my side;
Jon, 12,
sits on the rollaway cot
absorbed in Game Boy.

We are, all of us, measuring
the lengthening span
between my mother's breaths.
I am unaware of this
until Jon looks up from his Game Boy –
"It was 13 minutes that time, Mom."

Later friends encircle the bed,
their voices weave a container
that holds me steady,
allows me to release my grasp
on what I cannot hold.
My mother's hand, now mottled
feels cold and dry in mine.
Women's voices. Lois is telling a story.
She's almost to the punch line
laughter rings the room.
Jen says, "Look!"
and we stop.

My mother is white, still,
her final breath released.
She left on a wave of laughter.
We sit in silence.

Vivian, the nurse, comes
with her stethoscope
to pronounce the death.

Later, Lois helps me
wash and dress my mother.
Her limbs are loose and heavy.
I rub violet oil into her cold skin.
It scents the room.
We dress her for the fire:
her best tie-dyed T-shirt,
her purple pants.
I know Grace would like that.

Around midnight, the undertaker comes.
I help him zip the body bag.
I follow the gurney
out the front door to the death wagon,
watch the stretcher fold
and slide into the back.
The doors slam shut.
The undertaker drives away

I hear the full choir
of spring peepers
rising into the March night.

What Remains

I wake in the night
aware of my breath
remember
the last breaths
my mother took.

I wake with
a tear sliding
from the corner
of each eye
remembering
everything.

While the rushing waters
of daily life
sweep me along,
I return nightly,
pulled from the
warm trough of sleep
into her final days, hours
moments, into the land
of unrelenting questions.

What was that white puff
of mist she exhaled
not at the point of death,
but sometime before?
Does the spirit leave
by degrees?

How do we go on
when the landscapes
of our lives are altered
forever? How do
we embrace transition
and still grieve well?

At night I wake
knowing this:
the wheel of life
has turned again
leaving me
on the outer edge.

Kinds of Light

Northern Lights, green curtains
across the night sky,
fireworks, fireflies, campfires
none of them visible at noon.

Dawn and sunset,
the way they splash
color across the water,
ignite the horizon.

Last light in my mother's eyes
luminous as full moon
radiant beams
aimed straight at my heart.

Small Aches

The ones that wake me
briefly in the night
pulling me above
sleep's surface to lie
blinking in the dark.

The ghost pain
in my often sprained ankle,
beginnings of a headache
radiating from forehead
to behind my eyes.

I ache for family stories
that followed the elders
into silence,
regret questions never asked.
>What was Grandma Arnold's
>recipe for fried potatoes?
>Why did Great Aunt Carrie end
>her days in the Allentown State Hospital?
>Why don't I have more Grandpa John stories
>for the grandson he never knew?

When I see vultures soar
black against indigo,
hear great horned owls hoot
from deep in February woods,
I want to call my mother.
I always called my mother
with a nature report.
Her number
disconnected forever
a sharp-edged stone
in the bottom of my pocket
cuts my fingers
if I reach in too far.

The way
time hurtles at me
too fast
the way loss
like a heavy rock
pins me to the couch,
numb, voiceless;
the way my boy once
held his life close,
telling nothing,
hoarded his experience
like shiny pebbles
kept me in the dark.

The way movies
of my gone worlds
play behind my eyes,
the way memory
weaves a veil
between me and my life:
small aches.

Memories for the Next Thousand Years

My father's hands
hold a snake
he caught in the garden
or a cardinal he'd banded,
just before releasing
it to free flight.

Nana's voice hums
while she rolls out
pie crust,
or stitches
a quilt.

My secret spot
high in the white pine
above the house
above the yard
green and sticky
with pine sap,
the way the branches
softened the breeze
and sang with it.

The creek:
skipping stones
building dams
of clay, sand, pebbles:
first lessons
on the properties
of flowing water.

Bolts of love shoot
from my mother's
hazel eyes
into my heart
as she lies dying,
the way my being

catches and holds
the final beams
of her light
as she fades
into the spring night.

The Geography of Loss

Waking with dust
in my mouth,
pain in my heart,
I rise
to consciousness.

The reality of loss
develops slowly:
a Polaroid
of devastation
locks grief in
for the day
as first the edges
then the center
of the picture
come clear.

Vacant house,
one place setting
before an empty chair,
formless piles
of his clothing, folded.
Silence reverberates.

Desolate peaks rise
in murky distance
endless desert
sandstone arroyos
earth's bones exposed
by bitter wind.

This land
is full of dust.

Questions About Death

Suddenly I realize
if I step out
of my body
I might break into blossom
either that or the song
I am made of could stop.
Which is it?

What if it's both?
What if I bloom into a new form?
What if the song I am made of
changes tune and tempo?
What if the lyrics
rewrite themselves?
What if soul time begins
when the body clock stops?

When my old friend Brad
died last Thursday
in that car wreck
did he see his soul
unfold like petals?
Did he step out
from twisted metal,
broken glass
in one piece
singing his own song
at last?

Healing Song for Stephanie

for Stephanie Alston-Nero, friend and teacher, 1954-2016

Sister-in-spirit,
your bones are sharp
as the pain
that invades your body,
relentless as the doubt
that veils your mind.

You land for a moment
eyes intent
focus like a hawk
then soar again
beyond my vision.

I can hear the ancestors
calling in your voice,
hear their prayers
for deliverance
their song.
I see you standing
in the doorway,
your body a bridge.

Sister-in-spirit,
I hold you in light.
Let compassion and wisdom
lift your fear.
May the balm of love
soothe you,
ease your way
through.

Effects of Light

for H.S.

light alters
objects in its path
some souls alter us
when our paths
intersect

sometimes this shift
reverberates
across a lifespan
makes a bridge
between broken
and whole

when your soul
moved on
to the next world
two things happened:
 shadows fell
      across my path;
 a fissure opened
   in my heart
   spilling light

In the Apple Barrel Parking Lot

One month after,
I visit the scene of the limo tragedy.
Burnt out candles, photos,
mounds of frost-singed flowers,
a giant sawhorse holds
twenty wooden crosses
at the edge of the shallow ravine.

Twenty souls lost in minutes
when greed sends them down that hill
in a vehicle unfit for any road.
Brakes gone, they hurtle
through this parking lot,
take out two bystanders
and a Highlander, then
stopped dead
by that deep ditch.
Seventeen passengers,
and the driver,
gone in a blink.

Today tragedy waits,
stilled, dormant
as dead flowers
under thin November sun.

After the Tsunami

Devastation whispers,
slithers
over flattened villages.

Earth has spoken, her
desperate howls reverberate
through the ruins.

Hold hands,
weep, let heartbeats
find common rhythm;

let us shelter
under the tree
of Hope.

Questions

What happened to the lavender
dress I wore in that photo
when I was five? What happened
to the kittens in my arms?
Where do words go
after they leave our mouths?
Do they orbit forever with meteor
dust in deep space?

I used to hold my words
my memories close,
used to take them out
and count them, knew each one
like the shells and stones
I gather on journeys.
Now my memory card
is full: no more storage.
I have lost count.
How do leaves
know when it is time to
drop from the tree?
How do birds
know when to gather
on the wires
for the journey south?
Do the molecules in seawater
feel the tide change?

How much does a soul weigh?
Once a man told me
I weighed the same as
the color of gold;
now some days the air
dense as marsh mud,
clings to every surface
of my body
and I sink.

Other days my spirit
floats ahead, weightless,
iridescent as a bubble.
Can I hold
these questions
and still float?

Lunch 35 Years Later with the Man Who Broke My Heart

I know him, would know him anywhere
I see him first,
see him from the back
khaki pants, blue Oxford
button down shirt.
Will he know me?
Will he see the barefoot girl
at the edge
of a foggy wheat field,
remember who she was then,
who she still is
below the surface?

I see a tiny filament
an infinitesimally thin gold thread
worn but still gleaming
it connects us over distance and decades
unbroken.

We talk, drink iced tea,
trade family stories,
Beneath the surface,
edges of tectonic plates
grind and heave
rearrange
my interior landscape.

Now I am 17, 18, 19
in my 52 year old body,
I watch myself
eating chicken salad
like the grown-up middle aged woman
who walked into this restaurant,
know I will spend
the rest of my life wondering
if he saw the gold thread
too.

Where Time Goes

The song I still hear
is full of leaving
and changing seasons,
November geese calling
above the clouds,
sweet and melancholy
as a last kiss.

The song I still hear
calls forth creek walks,
a stucco house
on a hillside,
spreading maple tree,
cornstalks poking through snow.

The sweet sharpness
of the song I still hear
cuts through
the fog of now,
brings me back to
seventeen,
brings me back
to minute by minute
unfolding of stolen sweetness,
bursting bright then fading
fast as fireworks
against summer night.

The song I still hear pulls me
into memory's tide,
takes me away and brings me back,
leaves me on the far shore
of middle age
still wondering
where time goes and why.

Steel

after Coal, by Audre Lorde

I, silvery now, solid
done with pouring molten from the furnace
there are many kinds of strength
incandescent, iron flows, then cools
tempered into beam or blade
how words can become scalpels
whether the intent to wound or heal

some truths incinerate the spirit
how the crack of lightning singes air
splits pine, thunder merely an afterthought
there are truths that steal the breath
like a belly flop off a high dive
lungs squeezed flat struggle
to take in air again

some truths elude the brain
cluster like roaches behind baseboard
others erupt in a blinding flash
imprint on the retina like those
vaporized bodies at Hiroshima
images that can't be unseen
some truths
stick in my throat

connection becomes a casualty of truth
melts like iron in a blast furnace
I am silvery
tempered by the telling
incised
incinerated
strong as steel

Father

When I found out
the pilot was my father,
I did a vertical take-off.
Blew right past the wispy green
crowns of white pine,
ripped mist curtains off the mountains,
shot straight through thunderheads,
popped out into clear blue.

When I found out
my father was the pilot,
truth blew a hole in my history.
Lightning split
my family tree in two.
I sat dazed on damp earth,
picking through bark fragments
and splintered wood.

When truth blew a hole
in my history,
everything changed,
and nothing did.
I see them both now,
on the other side:
the gentle man who raised me,
the wild pilot
who buzzed our lives
in a P40 Thunderbolt

It took sixty-six years
for the sonic boom to reach me.

Longing

My ancestors' prayers
live in my blood.
Each droplet holds
the shadow of their fear,
their hope.

My birth is evidence
of love.
My life their leap
into the future.
My body holds
their bid for immortality.

I carry their history;
it has shaped mine.
My breath, my spirit
a bridge where
they stand now.

They wave to me
through the mist.

Time's Deluge

The clock's hands spin,
release a flood of memory.
Foamy torrents
rip through the day's landscape,
suck up bicycles, toolsheds, dog houses.
Look!—there's Jon's Little Tykes plastic climber
bobbing next to the wooden seesaws
from my first-grade playground.

I am witness to a tumbling museum.
Artifacts of lost childhood surface
and sink, one at a time.
All this churning generates
a great fog. Visibility
decreases to zero on the highway.
There are near misses, then pile ups-
burning tires, screeching metal.

Underneath the unrelenting symphony
of crashing cars and rushing water,
a space of silence vibrates
fast as hummingbird wings.

Prayer for the Transitory

for the curl of a perfect wave
rearing up green and gold
morning sun behind the crest
       Thank you

for spiderweb mandalas
silver coins on the June grass
that will be spent by noon
       Thank you

for my baby son's round cheeks,
his shiny eyes, his little fist
curled tight around a pinecone
       Thank you

for last night's sunset
coral against night's bottomless blue
November branches backlit in rose
       Thank you

for the cat who hunts
at field's edge
caught in the split second
of pre-pounce wiggle
       Thank you

for hurricanes forming,
strengthening, raging
then dissipating
for dark nights of the soul
and their surrender to light
       Thank you

nothing lasts
memory holds all
each moment has a half-life,
to be held

or released
      Thank you

Songline

• *Songline: (Australian Aboriginal mythology) A path across the land (or, sometimes the sky) marking the route followed by an Aboriginal ancestor made during the Dreaming which is often recorded in traditional songs, stories, dance and painting.*

not the old house, with flaking
paint, cracked plaster, purple door
not the long parade of cats and dogs

not the boxes of silver plated
flatware quietly blackening now,
in my barn, basement, attic;

but the white pine,
beech trees against blue sky,
jack-in-the-pulpit

the train trestle, me
walking the rails
the rhythm of refinery trains
crossing the lane twice a day,
once coming, once going

the hedge-row between pastures
thick with multi flora rose
where we guzzled beer
at midnight

full moon calling,
pulling me at fifteen from
a warm bed to stand
enthralled in frosty grass,
arms upraised

the noisy clouds
of blackbirds
blotting out twilight
on their way to roost

near the river

all of these
fit into memory's net
each one holds a note
in the songline
of my origins

Awake

When cold salt water
washes my feet,
I awake
know where I am.

When the long pull
of the moon
moving the ocean
draws me to the deep
or urges me to shore,
I know where I am.

When the osprey dives
fierce, focused
rises with a fish
clutched in her talons,

I wake
to my life again,
shocked into awareness.
This moment,
sharp, salt washed
is all I have.

Rites of Passage I

At sixteen,
I keep my fingers crossed
the day I leave for school,
first morning pee
hidden in
a brown paper bag.

In 1968 it takes
a whole week for results,
no simple wait to see
to see if a plastic stick
changes color in the privacy
of my bathroom.

I spend those days in
a haze of magical thinking.
I know what the results will be.
I call the doctor
from the school phone booth.
The nurse says
 "I have good news"

Nobody tells me
my breasts will swell
and ache and leak
after the abortion.
Nobody tells me how
to find my way out
of the pit.
I just keep digging.

Rites of Passage II

Five weeks after
the abortion,
held at knifepoint,
in an East Village apartment,
I realize how much
I still want to be alive.
It will take years
for the rape to register.
My fear of murder
makes the rape
incidental.

I sit in the wreckage
of my life.
Some days terrorized.
Other days blind with guilt.
Most days living.
anywhere
but in my body.

Summer 1966, Vietnam Conflict Escalates

What's left of that time
in my fifteenth summer
when I left my virginity
on the night beach in August
and was changed?

What's left are the snapshots
of me alone
at the railroad trestle,
sitting on warm blocks of stone
while red sun dropped
into a wheat field,
wood thrush trilling
damp, spice scented air rising
from the woods and creek below.

Another photograph
under the noon sun
the day I crossed
hand over hand,
a rock climber
clinging to the iron side
of the trestle
feet on the bottom ledge
sweaty hands holding hard
to the top ledge, edging my way
above the dirt road,
the little wooden bridge
the creek.

And what can't be seen
in any photograph: those moments
belonging to me alone, Bold,
crossing without a safety net.
            Fearless.
            Powerful.

Before I plunged
into Darkness:
> war in the world,
> war in me;
> before I became a casualty
> of my own choices.

There is no picture
of me on the bridge
> spread eagled between
> one section and the next
> grasping iron for dear life.

Once a Man I Loved

wrote poems for me.
No one before or since
ever wrote a poem with me in it.
I wonder what would have been
if I had allowed his words
to penetrate my frozen soul.

At seventeen I was
quiet on the outside,
one of the walking wounded,
survivor of assaults upon my person
and my spirit—at seventeen I was
a shook up, wrung out
don't know which end is up
kind of girl.

And yet when I saw those words
written just for me,
I felt something new in my blood.
Someone saw me as alive and whole
even after I'd left myself
for dead at the roadside.

Paralyzed, fear blind, I could not see
how that barefoot girl radiating beauty
at the edge of a wheat field
could possibly be me.

Now I see the rich gold wheat
feel the silky soil between my toes.
Now I catch the scent of leaves, and creek water
as they drift uphill with the mist.

Now I see the girl I was
infused with the richness
of the woman I have become.
I have not
forgotten any of it.

Death Speaks

from my SoulCollage® card

I am the one who
will come for you someday,
the one who will lead you
over the hills into the next life.

I am the ancient maple
rooted in bone and sorrow
who stands sentinel
over your father's grave.

I am the boat you must board
between known and unknown
and will take you
through to new territory.

I am the discordant note
in the music of your existence,
the one that makes you stop
and pay attention.

I am the signal that your ride
to the next place has arrived.
It is time to step into the carriage.

I will do this over and over
as time unrolls.
As you gather wisdom
you will learn to listen
for the first notes
of my call.

What Gets Us in the End

       not old age
       not dis-ease
but the weight
of our lost loved ones
finally bursting the walls
of our hearts.

Life carries
certainty of loss.
Death rides shotgun,
perched just above
the left shoulder,
always part of the journey.

Slippage

I am always forgetting
      something.
I forget appointments,
      keys
      what I went upstairs for.

I forget what I was doing
      when I heard
      Martin Luther King
      was murdered.
I forget all from that day
      except
      the dark hole
      ripped in my heart.

I lose track of time.
I can't think
      above the chatter
      of the news anchors,
      ministers of
      dis-information.
I forget to look at the sky.
I forget to drink
      from the well of gratitude.

I forget the touch of cool salt water
      on my breasts
      under moonlight.
I lose the threads.
      The fabric
      wears thin.
      Connections
      in the brain unravel.
I lose the sound
      of my father's voice,
      and the solitary song
      of the whippoorwill

singing me through
a sleepless night.

Finally, I remember
I dreamed a world
with no terror, no hunger,
no caged children.

Prayer for A Broken Land

~a shovel poem, using title "America, I Sing You Back,"
by Adelle Hedge Coke

I weep for my broken land. **America**
of charred canyons, red tides, your plagues of drought and deluge. **I**
weep to see it. I long to hear whales **sing**
as they migrate north. How can I bear to lose **you**,
how can I be still, struck silent while greed knifes you in the **back**.

I will stand up for you **America**,
beside the grandmothers and the waterkeepers. **I**
will stand up, will add my voice to those who **sing**.
I will plant my feet on earth and breathe **you**
whole again... With my breath, I call you **back**.

Broken cities, rusting junkyards, crumbling bridges, **America,**
you are my heart's home, the place **I**
have lived and where I'll **sing**
my death song. You have been my refuge. **You**
hold my dreams, my ancestors' bones. Please come **back**.

Litany for Survival

after Audre Lorde

for those of us steeped in privilege
wrapped in the invisible blanket of entitlement
unaware of our immunity
      if we believe in justice
      if our hearts hold compassion
we must own the inequities
that favor us
we cannot let this go unchallenged
our world balances on a sharp blade
we may be sliced in two
we are not meant to survive like this.

those of us who have not been
followed by a guard at Macys,
who have not been stopped
for driving while black,
who can pass through security,
walk down main street with ease
who wear no caste mark on our skin
must awaken
we are not meant to survive like this

when one more bullet
claims a life, we despair
when the one who aimed the Glock
is acquitted and hope pumps out
blood from a severed artery
we choke on outrage
and yet
it is not our child left fatherless,
not our family, our community
gazing into a crater whose emptiness
echoes up and down the generations
we don't know that sorrow

as the stink of slavery and genocide festers
under stained bandages
as we hear the grind of tectonic plates
colliding in LA, Detroit, Charlottesville,
we must stand up
embrace resistance
because none of us are meant to survive like this.

What I Want

I want the open sore
our country has become
to finish draining
and start healing.

I want children stolen at the border
returned to their mothers,
I want heartless bureaucrats jailed
with no parole.

I want kneeling
football players
awarded trophies
for honoring the fallen.

I want the ancestors
to gather, sing us songs
of solidarity,
stroke our brows while we sleep.

I want to see the homeless rise
from subway grates, park benches.
I want their empty bowls filled
with opportunity and blessing.

Just once,
I want to see billionaires
breaking bread with former felons,
single moms, runaways, bag ladies.

I want the mothers and grandmothers
to have enough time, enough money,
enough food to feed and nurture
all who come to the table.

I want to see reconciliation
trump racism. I want to see law

infused with love. I want
compassion as our currency.

The time has come
to balance the books,
clean the rivers,
heal our history.

Dark Days

Sometimes darkness
seeps into a day.
Filmy wisps gather,
thicken
into dense clouds
heavy with rain.

Sometimes in that pause
before rain, daylight
slips through clouds,
lights each leaf and petal
from within.

Sometimes it takes
a dark day
for me to find
my own light.

Silence

the silence after the last breath
has been released
the silence of the mushroom

the silence between
tripping and hitting the ground
the silence after the eulogy

silence after the unresolved argument
silence of an empty house
silence of boulders come to rest

after the landslide

Weight

Sometimes what
we don't say
fills up the air
between us.
The weight of it
makes it hard for me
to breathe.

Is it only
those of us
together for decades
who've mastered
the art
of arguing
without ever opening
our mouths?

Now and Then

his face turns from mine
after I speak

the tang of lime and garlic
infuses avocado's soft flesh

my father's hands
hold a chickadee

my mother's voice
the smoke from her cigarette
drifts in from a different room

the land that holds their ashes
grows thick with multiflora rose

Gates

after Jane Hirshfield

garden gate
trap door
barn door
ruined stone portal

some have hinges
some do not
one, stone rimmed,
frames the sea

winter's gate opens to dead cornstalks
October wind rattles chain-link
April dandelions sprout
through frost heaves

I have accompanied dear ones
to the gate between worlds
witnessed
the soul's departure

our souls too
hold portals
are doorways

deep in the body
a cell wall bursts
mitosis starts

deep in space
one star flares, collapses
births a worm-hole

a symphony
of swallowed light
numinous, the infinite

perhaps this perpetual
opening and closing
is the pulse
the under-song of all.

Judith Prest is a poet, photographer, mixed media artist and creativity coach. Her chapbook, After, was published by Finishing Line Press in 2019. Her work has appeared in Rockvale Review, Writers Resist (online), Up the River, Fredericksburg Literary and Art Review, Chronogram, Akros Review, Upstream, Mad Poets Review, Earth's Daughters and other journals, and in eight anthologies.

Judith worked for 26 years as a school social worker, and until the pandemic hit, worked part time for over 10 years at New Choices Recovery Center in Schenectady, NY, leading groups for Expressive Arts and Recovery Writing with adults in day treatment for addiction. She will continue to do creativity-and-healing retreats, creative writing workshops and expressive arts workshops, when gathering in public becomes safe again. In the past she has led workshops and retreats in prisons, retirement communities, conferences, libraries, schools, community agencies and at her home base, Spirit Wind Studio.

Judith was educated at University of Delaware and The Evergreen State College (BA), NY State University at Albany (MSW) and New York Expressive Arts Studio (Certificates in Creativity Coaching and Expressive Arts Therapy). Her mixed media art, paintings and photographs have been exhibited at several venues in the Albany area. She is a member of the International Women's Writing Guild, Hudson Valley Writers Guild, Foothills Arts Council and is a Poetry Partner with the Institute for Poetic Medicine.

She likes being anywhere in the woods, the mountains or by the ocean and hanging out with her cats. Judith lived in Bear, Delaware, Olympia, Washington and Jackson, Wyoming before settling in upstate New York and now lives in Duanesburg, NY with her husband Alan Krieger and the aforementioned cats, Ollie, Raven and Princess Leiah.

You can find her at judith@spiritwindstudio.net or on Facebook.
Website: www.spiritwindstudio.net